Jenny Oliver

HOPE

AUSTIN MACAULEY
PUBLISHERS LTD.

A CIP catalogue record for this title is available from the British Library.

ISBN 978 1 78455 164 3

www.austinmacauley.com

First Published (2015)
Austin Macauley Publishers Ltd.
25 Canada Square
Canary Wharf
London
E14 5LB

Printed and bound in Great Britain

Synopsis

I have been meaning to write this book for several years. Now that my children are adults, and have left home, I feel this is the right time.

I am the mother of two sexually abused daughters and possibly a son, and the victim of mental abuse towards me.

This is a story about my feelings and of the relationships I have with my children.

This would take over my life.

Even though my children were young, they would eventually tell me what had happened to them in their own individual way, and of the abhorrent things that had been done to them.

This story begins with a locked cupboard in a loft.

I discovered a blow up doll with 3 orifices, penis enlargers, complete with pubic hair, K-Y jelly, condoms and blue tights.

I went to the doctor for help and I was prescribed medication.

I then had to take my eldest daughter to the doctors as she had a vaginal discharge.

In view of my husband's depravity he thought my child had been sexually abused.

A vaginal swab was taken, which showed she had an anaerobe germ.

As had her father.

Things were now out of my control as social workers and paediatricians took over.

After further tests it was discovered that my daughters' hymens were intact.

Chapter One

I have been meaning to write this book for several years. Now that my children are adults and have left home, I feel this is the right time.

I am the mother of two allegedly, sexually abused daughters and possibly a son, by their father, and of the mental abuse I endured by my husband.

I talk about my feelings and of the relationships I have with my children.

During this time I had help from family and friends.

I had no support from others who had been through, or were going through this tragic experience.

As clichéd as this sounds I hope this book will help others and give them comfort in the knowledge that they are not alone.

This all began when my husband and I had a loft conversion.

In the loft there were cupboards along both sides and I had noticed there was a cupboard that was always locked.

I took the door off another cupboard and took this to a locksmith, who provided me with a key. I am not normally an inquisitive person, but this prayed on my mind as my husband was away at this time. When I unlocked the door I got the shock of my life.

Inside there was a blow up doll complete with three orifices, penis enlargers, vibrators complete with pubic hair – and there was only one place you could put that?

There were tubs of K-Y jelly and the largest box of durex I had ever seen.

My husband would later describe in great detail that he had to use condoms with the blow up doll otherwise there would be too much friction. Did I need to know this? He seemed to relish telling me as though this was normal.

I also found navy blue tights to finish this ensemble.

My first reaction was how would I put everything back, without my husband knowing what I had found.

By the time I had descended from the loft I felt very different.

I like to think I am broad-minded and that what happens in a sexual relationship, provided it is consensual, is fine However, I could not consent to what I had found – it was abhorrent to me.

This also explained why my husband, did not want a sexual relationship with me.

A friend of mine came round and together, within, half an hour put my husband's clothes and possessions in the garage.

The garage was adjacent to the kitchen so I could lock the door. I rang my husband's mother and told her what I had found.

She promised she would support my children and myself, and that was it.

I suppose I must remember it was her son. It then occurred to me that packages were sent to her home which I was asked to tell my husband to collect.

I never once questioned this, just passed on the messages. They were obviously his 'sex toys'. As you will see, this was the straw that broke the camel's back.

I then rang my absent husband and told him what I had found, and that our sham of a relationship was over.

I continued to find sex toys at the back of wardrobes.

I also found a letter to a dating agency describing himself as a handsome blue-eyed man; he is anything but.

Whether this was in the confines of our marriage, I don't know.

I felt broken and went to visit the doctor, due to the enormity of what I was going through, he prescribed Temazepam and amitriptyline.

These drugs would be part of my downfall.

Chapter Two

I had to take my eldest daughter to the same doctor as she had a vaginal discharge.

A swab was taken and the results showed she had an anaerobe germ, so did her father.

She was prescribed an anti-bacterial cream and I was advised to apply this to my youngest daughter's vagina. In view of my husband's depravity he felt my daughters had been sexually abused.

You will find something as innocuous as a tube of cream would play a part in my daughters' disclosures of alleged sexual abuse by their father. By this time the situation was now out of my control as paediatricians and social workers took over.

The paediatrician took further vaginal swabs and my daughters were medically checked.

I was told by social workers that "that man should not see his children". I was in a state of shock, I didn't know how to cope or who or where to turn too.

It was like living in a total daze; that this wasn't happening to us.

It was like falling down a black hole, there was no way out.

How could I not blame myself? How could I not have known? What was happening under my very nose? How could have I not seen the signs? Some people will say, "She must have known", but the sad truth is that I didn't.

How can the human mind comprehend such atrocities a paedophile is capable of? The truth is we can't.

My daughter was five years old.

To this day my ex-husband has felt no remorse against his "alleged paedophilia" or his "inappropriate behaviour". This is his sexual preference, his nature, and like any addict he could not stop. I wrote a poem around this time, I have left it how it was written at the time.

'Sometimes I feel like my teddy bear, worn out and patched and nearly threadbare.

I have a line here, I have a line there, like my Teddy bear, who is nearly threadbare but, when you look, she is still all there, cuddly and safe, is my old teddy bear.

Because she doesn't judge she loves you just as you are because after all she is my teddy bear.

But, when you are too old and it's too late to change even though you try, there is no one there, except my teddy bear.

And when you feel calm and have that peace.

You can only thank my old teddy bear.

She's the one I trust, the only one there, is my old teddy bear.

She gives you hope even though there is no one there and, when you can't sleep because of troubles there, I just need to think of my old teddy bear.'

I was 31.

Chapter Three

It breaks my heart to realise I was a pawn in my husband's game, the game was over, he had won.

I had been used for his own ends. I felt my children deserved better, I deserved better. I had never questioned what my children had told me. They were the innocent. In so many cases I have read the mother calls the child a liar or that they led the perpetrator. This is inconceivable to me.

My daughters knew things about sex that they should not know or every have to deal with. Our children are not sex objects to be displayed and discarded at will.

They should stay young and naive, their minds uncluttered by adult things and certainly not have to deal with a sexual predator.

We cannot forget that children are coached from a young age, as were mine, which I will discuss later.

I felt bad as I had not protected my children from my ex-husband.

My thoughts were totally consumed with what my two young daughters were telling me about their father I have read hundreds of books about child abuse I have seen so many films and there is always something I can relate to.

One thing that comes to mind is the "Wrestling game" whereby the person leans over the child pinning their arms over their head and gyrates. In my children's case this was put down to "inappropriate behaviour", by their father.

Another game my ex-husband played was the "horsey game".

Where he would bounce my daughters upon his knees I had always let my ex-husband have a bath with my children and thought nothing of it. I let the children run around the house naked and thought nothing of it.

I didn't think 'child abuse' cubes why should I? It is so hard to believe a person can do these depraved things. There is no understanding or logic to it.

You cannot believe this barbarity exists and is perpetrated even on young babies.

Were my babies abused or were they older? I don't know and will never know, but what I do know is that paedophiles exist and they live among us. They look no different they act no different – or do they? And it is conceivable that you may be married to an alleged paedophile.

The paedophiles to me are lower than animals.

Paedophiles are intelligent and manipulative.

They coach children and they know how to protect themselves so that they can continue to abuse. Paedophiles seek out the vulnerable, the gullible and weak.

Just like me. There is one thing I do know for sure, he had me exactly where he wanted me, and he had my children exactly where he wanted them.

Chapter Four

My children were put through so much; invasive medical checks, having vaginal swabs, being watched whilst they were playing. My ex-husband and I were watched for how we interacted with them.

They were seen by a top paediatrician, the best in the country.

Apparently my ex-husband made paper aeroplanes and threw them around the room.

This was seen as fun. When I was watched my eldest daughter asked what shall I do? I suggested that I would draw a clown and she should colour this in.

This was seen as leading, and that I was a needy mother.

It beggars belief.

Throughout these interviews with social workers and paediatricians my children made no reference to the fact that they had been "allegedly" sexually abused, they at this time chose only to tell me.

Most people know that children "don't tell". They don't like what is happening to them but, they don't know why.

It is also known that a child can be battered and bruised by their parents yet they still love them.

Children can be told that they wouldn't be believed, and threatened, that their mother may be harmed, and they might never see their mother again, and who knows what else.

There is only one person who knows, the paedophile, and he is not letting on.

My daughters were pulled from pillar to post.

And still they did not say anything to the professionals. As these interviews progressed, my eldest daughter, as she was videoed, which I was able to watch, said something so abhorrent.

It stays firmly embedded in my brain.

After a while I had to leave the room.

Chapter Five

My eldest daughter disclosed that her father took her to his bedroom and locked the door.

He took his trousers off and put his willy near her face.

The doorbell rang, he got dressed and went to answer the door.

She then ran into the bathroom and washed her face with a flannel I was so upset I had to leave the room.

When I am upset for some reason my throat makes a noise, this is like a gurgling sound, it was affecting what the social worker was hearing.

I don't know what else she said I wasn't told. This was still 'inappropriate behaviour'.

There was one night my youngest daughter couldn't sleep.

She wanted to colour and write a story, she drew a picture of herself and wrote "Daddy puts cream on my tuppy, whether it is sore or not".

She was five years old.

My ex-husband jeopardised my children's innocence all because he could not control his selfish and overwhelming drive to allegedly sexually abuse my children.

My daughter would draw this picture and the same words over and over again and show her grandma and her aunt.

I showed the social worker, nothing ensued. To try and get support for myself I used to visit the doctor to tell him what my children were telling me, once he said, "we are fed up hearing about this". I can't understand or respond to this comment. It made me feel even more alone. I lived in my own kind of hell.

Which resulted in a seven year breakdown.

I hadn't realised at the time, but looking back I can see this plainly.

I stopped looking after myself, I wore pyjamas all the time, I stopped cleaning my teeth.

I did have a shower and wash my hair, I wore no makeup and didn't look in a mirror. I became obsessed with cleaning and painting the house.

I painted anything that didn't move.

Everything had to be gold and silver. I painted furniture, floors and even the bath.

I painted the doors continually even painting the doors after my children had left for school.

It was madness, I was manic.

I felt I had to fill in every waking minute of my life, so I didn't have to think about what was happening to my family.

I desperately wanted to sleep as this caused oblivion, but I knew what could happen whilst I was asleep. If I was awake, no harm could happen to my children, if I was asleep it could.

It was like a double-edged sword.

I was unable to function in society, I was inept.

I could not cope and sadly I never could again.

I think as my daughter grew we dealt with our demons alone, which is so sad.

I have tried so hard to move on and find peace.

But then something happens again relating to the alleged abuse that makes me take one step forward and one step back.

Which I will explain later.

Chapter Six

Before we were married my husband's hand was always there, holding mine, he was attentive and caring.

There were some 'niggles' which would eventually turn into big ones. He didn't seem to like sex as much as me.

He would take me out for a drink, and not speak throughout. Then he would turn up at tea time as though nothing had happened. I brushed these worries aside, I loved him. After about a year into our marriage, he changed.

He virtually ignored me, mentally and sexually.

He spent the majority of his time in the spare bedroom or loft.

He had never once said "happy birthday" to me.

I was deprived of having a happy marriage, I was deprived of having a loving father for my children, I was deprived of bringing them up in a two parent family.

It is amazing that you can make one wrong decision, one mistake, and that would make your life spiral out of control and plummet into hell.

My mother always said heaven and hell are here on earth. She was right.

The blow up doll and his sex aids, the alleged abuse of my daughters, no one could predict that.

I had been through my marriage without love or support.

Although my husband wasn't a violent man he abused me in other ways. He used hurtful and spiteful words, he withdrew from me physically.

Later, he produced his penis which was covered, in sores with the herpes virus, he had caught abroad when he had had a one night stand.

Would it have made a difference if he had told me?

Yes, I think it might have, but he didn't. Once I went eighteen months without sexual contact.

I, of course, blamed myself.

I wasn't pretty enough, I wasn't interesting enough, his behaviour crushed me and I had a long way to crawl out of the hole he had thrown me in. The one he eventually dug for himself.

Consequently, I built up my own life around my children and friends.

I opened a children's nursery and I started child minding. My friends started taking me out socially and little by little I started to live life again with devastating consequences.

I was so wrapped up in my own misery it was years before I wondered if he had done this to the other children. He certainly had the opportunity. My daughters' friends often stayed for sleep overs. Did he have images on his computer? Did he have a lock on the door as my eldest daughter had told me? Social services never checked.

When my ex-husband was allowed to see my children again, albeit with supervision with his mother, this was no way forward.

Around this time my ex-husband took my children to a professional photographer, twice.

I believe these photographic sessions cost a lot of money.

There were poses of my daughter in Basques with one arm above her head, and one of my son with his shirt pulled over his shoulder.

Is that considered normal? I think not.

He showed me these images rubbing his hands in glee.

In view of his alleged paedophilia would I have looked at these in a different way? I don't know, but I think not.

My children had copies of these but my ex-husband had more.

Chapter Seven

I love my children unconditionally, I have written about their demons and some of mine.

I would eventually lose my eldest daughter to her father at age fourteen.

I would eventually lose my youngest daughter at age sixteen to her father.

I felt they were walking into the lion's den, I was proved right.

I could do nothing about this, he could see his children.

Just before my youngest daughter moved she said, I have a vaginal discharge from when "my daddy touched me", I asked her if her father was doing this, she replied, "don't be disgusting", I spoke about this with my sister and we both talked to my daughter, she said, "mammy told me to say this".

I find it interesting that she reverted back to saying mammy and daddy.

Because of my inability to keep my mouth shut I told a friend about this, she in turn told her daughter, who in turn told a mutual friend, both then talking to my daughter about this.

And it was this reason that she wanted to move.

And it was all my doing.

Around this time I had noticed she was spending a long time over the phone, speaking to her father as I later found out she would take the phone into the bedroom and close the door.

I then received a phone call from my daughter's school, asking did I know that my daughter had been looking to move schools to where her father lived.

I did not, this broke my heart, and it had all been down to me.

When her father came to collect her, she sat on his knee like a small child, with him patting her.

I felt sick to the stomach.

He had promised her a laptop, clothes, shoes, in fact all manner of things.

He had bought her; we cannot forget that my children had probably been coached from a young age, as this will be seen later on in the book.

Also, we cannot forget as I believe, to abuse his own flesh and blood again, he made my skin crawl.

As I write this book memories keep flooding back to me, if this reads a bit jumbled I apologise for that.

Also in writing this I am feeling a lot of emotions, anger, sadness, I could go on and on.

Once my husband donned a pair of my leggings I was so shocked I was rendered speechless.

Was he homosexual? Was he a cross dresser? I can't answer that and the secret stays with him.

When you don't know the answer to things your mind can run riot, there are so many 'what ifs and what buts' you could send yourself mad which sadly I did.

Another obsession of mine was writing and illustrating children's books, I have written at least forty, it is very different writing a 'true life' novel. Many abused children have written about their lives and some have beaten the odds, becoming worthy functional human beings.

But what happens to those who don't? Do some go on to be abusers themselves? Do some self-harm and take drugs?

How are these poor souls now?

There is so much child abuse in this world that it hurts we are hearing more about this as adults come forward and tell us of their abuse as children what can we do to help children disclose earlier? And when they do, do adults believe them as I believed my children.

Paedophilia is certainly more out in the open now, and I believe in name and shame, but these animals go underground and amass together to abuse children.

We also hear about physical abuse, how can we stop this? This abuse is also beyond our comprehension Signs are seen by social workers, but as in my case not enough is done.

Do these children have to die, before help is available? It seems that some do.

Chapter Eight

From a young age my eldest daughter had difficulty swallowing.

I took her to the doctor who could find nothing medically wrong. By nature she had to swallow, but this caused her severe distress.

She was three. Also, she had a problem going to the toilet for a poo.

Again I went back to the doctor who again said nature would take its course.

Which it did, but this would hurt her more as the bowel would become impacted.

She would scream in agony.

I started singing to her "push that poo down the loo, just where it should be."

I tried to make her laugh, in fact I tried anything I could think of, but I could not help her.

She was four.

Later on she would soil her underwear rather than use the toilet. She would do this in front of family and friends.

I found this incredibly hard to deal with, luckily my mam was incredible.

She had wanted to join the Guides but this problem hindered her.

She was 9 years old.

As my daughter grew up she began telling me things that no child should know, for instance, her dad had a tool box of toys under his bed.

She didn't like this game.

At night time she and her sister would wait and hear their father's footsteps on the stairs, both wondering "which one would go with daddy". There were signs of oral sex.

I have mentioned more later on in the book. At age 14, she wanted to go and live with her father, she was abusive at school, swearing at the teachers setting alight paper in the class room. This was one very sad little girl.

By this time her father was able to see his children.

She had told me all the things her father had promised, if my daughter wanted it, she got it.

My darling daughter had been bought.

As a single person I struggled financially, I hadn't taken my ex-husband to court over maintenance, I just thought he would pay, but he never did.

He was laughing at me, again.

My daughter left with her brother, without a wave goodbye, I was bereft.

She had gone.

Whilst living with her father she began to take drugs and getting into trouble with the police.

She would ring me crying her heart out, scared of what might happen.

I lived miles away, I couldn't help her. I could only listen.

I had let her down again, I didn't have the money to go and get her.

Her aunts on her father's side lived near, I was comforted by this; they loved her and I knew they would help.

A while later my daughter rang to say she was gay.

I knew that when she had been born that she was gay.

I loved my daughter and this didn't bother me in the slightest, but what did bother me was how others might treat her; I loved her so much, it hurt.

Around this time she began to run away, her father if he hadn't had a drink would go and fetch her.

Otherwise she was on her own.

She also started using my surname. The school rang me about this, but accepted it.

My sweet daughter began to self harm, she became very angry, on one occasion punching a wall breaking her fingers. Looking back, she was always angry and I feel it was this that triggered her behaviour.

Another stage she went through was not washing herself or her hair.

Her lack of hygiene was noted where she worked at the time.

I believe she received a warning.

Also, I have heard of this before.

These poor children don't want attention; they make themselves as unattractive as they can.

To repel human contact.

My daughter has now moved on, she has a good job and is studying for a Degree.

It seems her self-harm, drugs and anger are behind her, unlike her sister, who is still struggling. I hope and pray that that is so, I hope she stays well and happy, which is all I want for her.

Chapter Nine

One night my youngest daughter could not sleep she asked if she could draw a picture and write a story. I said "yes", I wondered what would have happened if I had said no? My daughter drew a picture of herself in blue and pink and wrote "daddy touches my tuppy with or without cream". I had used the word tuppence to describe her vagina.

Throughout all of this she didn't disclose as much of the alleged abuse as her sister.

She would show her picture and story to her family, friends, social workers and paediatricians. Nothing was acted upon.

Once my daughters lay top to toe, I asked what they were doing, my youngest daughter said, "daddy does this, why can't we?" I did not have the answer to that one.

She was five.

My second daughter had always been small and thin, when the school weighed and measured her she was always under height and weight on the Percentile chart.

I never questioned this, as a child I was the same, I am only 5' 4". However, I did notice she wasn't eating much, I was met with the excuse that she had eaten a lot at school, and was going out to eat with her friends. I just accepted this and thought no more about it.

This was the onset of anorexia, and I hadn't known I remember my son saying, "What kind of mother are you?"

This didn't help my self-esteem, but he was right.

I should have known about this, and of the alleged abuse, but I didn't. It had broken my heart and it was all my fault.

I could hardy live with myself.

My second child excelled at school and at university and excelled at her two Masters degrees; I was so proud I could burst.

During her first Masters degree she came back to live with me, I was delighted; it was a special time for me.

During these two years I discovered that my daughter was self-harming, and at the time it seemed like she was slashing herself. She also planned to commit suicide several times resulting in a hospital stay where she had stomach pumps fits and seizures Throughout this time her brother was by her side day and night and he witnessed all of this.

She never wanted me to be with her I wondered if she had been doing this.

Had she been doing this when she lived with her father, or at university? I don't know, but I think so.

I found it hard to understand self-harm, at first I thought it was to see the blood, but later I realised it is done to cause pain, to hurt themselves, I also know that it is not attention seeking, it is an illness and like any addiction she has to overcome this herself, I can only watch.

My, daughter has terrible scars on her wrists and hips, some quite deep.

My daughter tries to cover her scars up with wide bracelets and bio oil.

Had she self-harmed or tried to commit suicide when she lived with her father, and at university, I don't know, but I sensed that she had, she never told me and I never asked.

Recently whilst on holiday with her father and aunts, she had slashed her wrists and hips.

My poor daughter is punishing herself over and over, she is the innocent in all of this; nothing was her fault.

She did come to me twice when she had cut her wrists quite badly.

I had to call the ambulance; they treated the wounds and admitted her to hospital.

She didn't want me to go, but she let my sister go with her, which I was glad of, but I was sad that she hadn't wanted me.

I also noticed she had been drinking far too much, and this fuelled with anti-depressants can be a lethal combination, alcohol is a depressant.

There is I believe something called the Stockholm syndrome, a psychological phenomenon whereby victims feel sympathy towards their abuser, when the abuser is not being violent or aggressive it is perceived that lack of abuse as kindness and the victim forms a traumatic bonding.

Is this true in my daughter's case? it certainly seems so, but I am not an expert.

Chapter Ten

I had a marvellous relationship with my son as a boy. I adored him as I did his two sisters.

As he grew into his teens a lot changed between us.

He was a typical teenager going out, drinking too much. He brought his friends around for parties. My mam used to say, "If he is at home, at least you know where he is". I liked a lot of his friends but these parties used to get out of control.

I liked some of his friends, getting very close to a couple.

Having said that, I was not respected, neither was my home.

Some of my furniture and possessions were broken.

There were no apologies.

The parties had to end. My son told me he didn't respect me and never had.

He could be very hurtful and I found it hard to understand why? I loved him so much and tried to do everything I could for him.

If I am in a room he wants to use, I have to leave it.

My children have so much animosity towards me and it hurts.

I have no alternative but to carry on, but I am always sad.

As far as the alleged sexual abuse towards his sisters is concerned he was young and I never spoke to him about it.

As far as I know my eldest daughter told him, he was nine.

My children have had a rough start in life and I don't blame them for it.

My son's father didn't treat him as kindly as his sisters, even his cousin got presents when he did not.

I remember this vividly. The girls got a small skate board. He did not.

The girls got Winnie the pooh pillows. He did not. This must hurt, but at the end of the day I am not responsible for the way his father treats him.

To my knowledge he was never tempted by his father to live with him, as my girls had been. Did being a boy make a difference? However, in arguments he threatened to do so, but we all say things we don't mean.

All my son said regarding the alleged sexual abuse was that he had spikes in his poo. I took this to mean it hurt him to go to the toilet.

As he turned into a young man his bitterness towards me remained.

In view of this I told him about the abuse towards me and what I had found in the loft.

I vowed never to tell my children about this but I was at my wits end and hoped this would help him understand.

I realise now it was a very selfish, self-centred act on my behalf and I regret it to this day, but at that time I felt justified in doing so.

My son went very quiet and made me promise not to tell his younger sister.

Unfortunately my eldest daughter knew.

Her cousin had told her, I was very upset about this and had not realised that he knew. But he did and there was nothing I could do about it.

My son had witnessed his sister's attempted suicides; he had seen her cut herself and the aftermath that ensued.

At hospital he was there when his sister had stomach pumps, the fits and seizures.

As my daughter didn't want me there, I was grateful that my son never let her side.

As my son left home to start a new life with his girlfriend, I cried my heart out.

He was my last child to leave home. It didn't make any difference at the time that he was moving down the road.

I hope one day that he realises how much I love him, and all I wish is that he is happy and as well as when he threw a paper aeroplane.

As my son left I had a phone call from my daughter.

She told me she had cut herself quite deeply, and had not eaten for a while.

Her anorexia had returned.

Chapter Eleven

The first social worker I met was absolutely marvellous; I felt supported and was made to feel that my daughters and myself mattered.

Her first words were, "that man must not see his children", she worked hard with my daughters, but they didn't have the words to explain what had happened to them.

It would be a few months before my young daughters would start disclosing what had happened to them.

They were 5 and 3.

In view of the situation we found ourselves in, I decided to move away and live near my sister and her husband, who stated, "get them up here, now", my ex-husband couldn't deny us this as he was now in a vulnerable position. A new social worker was attached to the case.

She was relentless.

She barraged me with questions week after week, delving deep into my past, sending me to a very dark place.

I was told it was wrong listening to my daughters.

I was told it was wrong to ask my children about the alleged abuse, I was wrong about everything, and didn't she let me know it.

At five month's old I had been adopted, I have never had any desire to find my biological parents.

I was happy with the mam and dad I had, strangely I worry what could have happened if they had not adopted us.

My father asked his supervisor for a day off work, he was asked "why" and my father told him he was bringing home his twin girls.

He lent my father his chauffeur and limousine as my father did not have a car at that time and would have to take a bus.

We arrived in style.

My twin and I are fraternal, we differ in looks, and in fact we are different in every way.

Strangely, if I am honest I had never wondered if we had any siblings until my sister mentioned it.

I have never thought of my biological father.

I don't have issues about this and never had.

But, my social worker had different views over this.

Everything closed in on me like a pack of cards and the issue she had with my adoption was intense.

It just came crashing down on me.

I became confused as to why my life was so important to her. I have never felt such injustice my ex-husband was also questioned, the only thing I found out about this is that he is a mummy's boy.

I felt like a wild animal backed into a corner, and for the life of me I didn't know why. Whilst this was ongoing my ex-husband could not see my children.

What upset me the most was that no one checked his bedroom for a lock, which my eldest daughter told social worker's about.

His computer was never checked; neither did they medically check my son. They never even wondered if he had abused any more children, in fact social services were a dead loss.

The mammy's boy had convinced social workers that nothing had happened between him and his daughters, and everything was put down to "inappropriate behaviour".

What?

He was now able to see my children, albeit supervised.

The first time he took my children out, he was over two hours late bringing them back to me. I was frantic. The supervisor was blasé and explained the traffic was bad, in a jolly way my ex-husband and social worker laughed as they walked towards my front door. I was speechless.

I could never understand why social workers didn't take seriously the disclosures my eldest daughter made on the video recordings.

Why didn't they take the anal scanning and the unusual skin folds that had been medically found? As it was anal abuse, why hadn't the checked my son? All of this and more was put down to "inappropriate behaviour"? I dread to think what has to happen before sexual abuse is discovered. If I ever see that social worker again I would slap her face, and say … "Look at my daughters now, look what you have done. Look what you have done to our family."

You have sent my daughters and my son straight back to the alleged perpetrator.

It seemed to me that they were working together, yet at the same time she put me on the 'at risk' register. The injustice beggars belief.

Chapter Twelve

This is the penultimate chapter in this book.

My ex-husband took me to court for custody of my children.

I had written about the alleged abuse from the onset, I passed this on for my solicitor to read, who then passed it to the judge.

I was so nervous, I shook from head to foot; my words faltered and I could not find the passages that I was referring to.

A clerk kindly helped me.

I was due back in court the next day.

When I returned to court the following day I knew I had the fight of my life on my hands, I couldn't lose my children, I was their mother.

And I did fight, and I fought well.

Unbeknownst to me my father had just caught my solicitor on his way to another hearing.

He told the solicitor that my mother would live with me indefinitely if needed.

This was passed on to the judge.

The judge had a near impossible decision to make, did he award custody to an alleged paedophile or an alcoholic, myself, or place my children in care?

If my father hadn't spoken to the solicitor, I could have lost custody of my children. If my mother hadn't lived with me I would have lost custody of my children.

But, custody had been awarded to me.

I could not thank my parents enough, without them I would have lost.

How can anyone repay a debt like that? Not forgetting my father had to live without his wife for several months; my mam died over a year ago and I like to think I have paid her back, I promised her I would never drink again, and I haven't, I have been sober now for over 17 years. I also like to think I have paid my father back as well. I wrote about my mam's death, which you can read, dedicated to the incredible lady that she was.

This is the lady I am proud to call my mam who went over and above in her unconditional love for me.

I have no words to truly express my gratitude.

Just an overwhelming love for her, and not forgetting my dad who had supported me throughout

My mam she died in dad's arms just as it should be.

I will remember my mam when the breeze rustles the leaves and they crunch under foot.

I will remember my mam when I hear a giggle or a laugh. My mam lives on in my heart and soul, at night she sleeps with angels and watches over me.

I will love my mam until my dying day, where she waits for me, arms outstretched just as it should be.

Hello, Mam, here we are in our final resting place, you can hear the children laughing and playing in the park.

Birds are singing overhead. You are with me in my heart and soul and I know you are with me.

When everyday life's little coincidences remind me of you.

And I say, "Hello, Mam".

Here we are one year on and I miss you just as much.

Here we are one year on and my heart aches just as much.

Here we are one year on when we held you close, as you said your last goodbyes.

Here we are one year on and the leaves are falling all around me in an autumnal cascade, crunching underfoot reminding me of you.

Here we are one year on and the changing colours of autumn remind me of you, keeping me safe and giving me solace knowing you are all around me, loving me.

Here we are one year on and I know I will see you again, in that special place you have saved for me.

Chapter Thirteen

I now need to write about my "dark secret", one time alcoholic would have been put in the closet and forgotten about, but I have not had a drink for seventeen years and I am proud of myself for that.

Whilst I was trying to build my shattered life, I started to drink again. Not heavily at first, but it wasn't long before my drinking was out of control. Combined with prescription drugs sometimes it rendered me unconscious.

And that was where I had wanted to be, I couldn't think then.

I have written a book about this, but I need you to know, in order for you to understand me.

I had put myself in the exact place my ex-husband wanted me.

I had played right into his hands. When I had my first daughter I wanted to look after her myself, but financially I could not.

I held down a good job in the civil Service. And I was able to go part time.

Eventually I built up a children's nursery and coupled with money from child minding I was able to leave the civil service.

I loved looking after my daughter and two years later I had a second daughter. After two years I longed for another child, and I had a lovely boy.

I felt my family was complete.

There was one problem: I was mainly ignored by husband and seemed to be looking after my children alone.

After the rejection by my husband, I felt ugly which I still feel today. I felt I was unlovable, I still feel that today. I was not interesting enough, I still feel that today. I was not intelligent enough, and I still feel that today.

As it dawned on me that I would get no help from my husband. I just had to get on with things. I had some lovely friends who had been with me throughout.

Things settled down as much as they could, only my life had changed forever, my ex-husband started to take bottles of wine around to my best friend's house, I don't know what they talked about, she never told me.

He also spent time at another friend's house and went out drinking with him.

My ex-husband started going out with a girl my friend knew, spending a lot of time at her house, which meant that I could not go.

I could not believe what was happening.

I was ousted.

Both these friends had been with me on hospital visits with my daughters, to the paediatrics, and visits with social workers. My ex-husband is an alleged paedophile; one of them had even "kept my children safe from him"? When I asked about this our friendship ended.

I had done everything for my friend, I gave her a job at my nursery, and I drove her wherever she wanted to go, but in the blink of an eye, I was alone.

I am now in a deep depression, no one would help me with my nursery, I drank too much, and due to my alcoholism and I lost my beloved nursery.

I had done all this myself, I lost everything I loved, I just functioned like a robot, taking my children to school, feeding them clothing them, but that was it I took medication and drank alcohol with what could have been lethal consequences.

Basically I opted out of life, it didn't care about me, I didn't care about it.

I functioned in taking my children to school, feeding them and clothing them, but that was it.

I had lost, and my ex-husband was laughing.

I took medication and drank, I basically opted out of life.

It was just too hard, life didn't care about me, and I didn't care about it.

I had to live with the fact that I had done this to myself.

I was playing straight into my ex-husbands hands and he was laughing.

The fact that I had done all this myself was hard to live with.

I was at rock bottom where there is only one way to go and that is up.

I moved to live near my sister, my dad bought me a house, and we set off for a fresh start. Only it wasn't a fresh start.

I had started drinking again with a vengeance.

My mother and father left their home and moved to be near me so they could help.

The truth is no-one can help, I had to do it myself but I couldn't.

Everyone, my sister my mother and father, helped with the children while I lay comatose wherever I fell. Once again if my family hadn't helped, I would have lost my children.

But drink takes over and sadly that is all important. nothing else mattered, not even my children.

Eventually my dad had found out about a group you visited daily. It dealt with addicts or all sorts.

This was the first time I encountered "self-harming", my father drove me there and back.

This didn't work at first, but by the time I left, I was sober, and I have stayed that way ever since.

I believe the group has been closed due to lack of funds which is such a shame.

Conclusion

This may sound harsh but I don't have the power to forgive.

Perhaps I need to in order to move on.

If this book is published I want to be as honest as possible. So here goes.

In view of all that has happened I hope what goes around comes around.

I have an intense feeling of hate and I want to name and shame.

I want him to take the consequence of his actions, his 'inappropriate behaviour'.

So the children can move on.

They deserve no less.

I want my daughters to value themselves; their bodies were not there to be used at will, and then discarded.

I accept and apologise for the damage I have inflicted on my children due to my drinking.

I have atoned by my never drinking again, and I haven't. My children were aged 5 years, 7 years and 9 years at the time.

My daughters are precious, as is my son. We have all been to hell and back because of his 'inappropriate behaviour'.

Is he still behaving like this? I don't know, but what I do know is that he is now a 57 year old pathetic man.

My drinking had been an excuse for everything that had happened and I had walked straight into that trap.

As for me, I will never be the same again and sadly no amount of therapy can change that.

Addendum

Whilst trying for my first baby my husband said it made him feel sick.

When I brought my new born son home, my husband was in the garden sun bathing. As I passed by he was talking to my friend about 'sniffing knickers' my mother was in the kitchen looking after his son.

He had always joked about bottoms which I had found obnoxious, he seemed to be obsessed about this.

When my eldest daughter had broken her arm whilst in his care, he asked me which hand she used to wipe her bottom with? He said this in glee whilst rubbing his hands together.

He gave my dog an onion to see (in his words) if he would fart and proceeded to laugh about it.

At the same visit he bought food for my children and himself and ate it in front of me.

I was ignored in my own home.